# AUTUMN GUILT MECHANISM

**poetry by**
**Jess Boldt**

The author wishes to thank the editors of the following publication
for printing a previous version of a poem in:
Confluence: spring 2003 "A Love Poem for Everyone" now titled
"Apply Sarcasm"

Jess Boldt  P.O. Box 15314 Fort Wayne In, 46815

ISBN   978-0-6151-3774-2

1st edition

The author wishes to extend sincere gratitude to friends. I would also like
to thank Abby W. for her help with the formatting of the cover.  I would
also like to give sincere thanks to the girl for whom I rushed through a test
just for an opportunity to catch her in the hallways.
contact the author at jessboldt@gmail.com
www.drunklikeleaves.com

# Table of Contents

For my mother, Alana
for all the support

## Last Ditch Drainage

I only see white cars
when we rested
drunk like leaves
stuck in
pre-frost
dirt

Flooded libido
A simple guilt mechanism
where autumn changed
motions leading
us to skin
sedative sleepy

## Apply Sarcasm

Don't start
with this again
puppy face whimper
A weekend of nursed up
sounds break familiar, unfair

Are you searching for a light
underneath a drunkard's bed

More inclined to lay back
watch the smoke
from a flickered out
matchbook

Tempted
to tease here for
something more interesting
but she is boring regardless
The only light may just be
the one in your fridge

**For**

Wait up the stairs
crash back onto
mirror vase landmines

notice glass cut
reflection warps itself
into flowing red pageantry
keeping yourself chaste
alert and taunt


hormonal hostilities
they don't waste time
with sarcastic smiles
and chocolate melt
warm hands

moist throned devils
with bee sting intentions
drop kick
football fanatics
that keep going
like halved worms
after the shovel cut

don't expect a

savior detour
rampage raging light
you will just turn it away

This will happen

pt. 1
(outside)

I like her because she leaves at 2am
       engine sounds
          lull into unconsciousness

## Trainbound Out

Upward bending
amongst grey
lined pillars
Triumph over
twilight civilizations
A route in progress
Jet lag shoes tap their
soles on kinetic
marble sidewalks
pulled body
by wings of
ghosts
clamped well
into the shoulders

Effort spins slow
Gliding bed bound
until the
tips of leather leaves
earth

Behind it drops
the recollections
of neighbors
too busy to
tether

## Karma Lingo

Your promise delivers
substance to an alarm
and clicks inside of me
inside of something

Whispers to pass the time
and thoughts of shy passed
doodles scratched on
clinched napkins, tabletops

50 cents per word
structures  into paragraphs
structures into books
never written

Each attempt lined up
before our mistakes and
thrown into caste
displayed in
the rear view
to laugh at

the price of self judgment

We cling to each other like wet leaves against
window pane

everything clings

for awhile

## Nitrogen Psychosis

Induce the innocent
to become like snow bunnies
hop around without
need of masks
white powder trails
constantly cleansing the past
acrobatic smiles
assuming a softer ground
will catch their fall

How do they do that without a net?

## Crush Can

it starts something
shadow skin beneath
perception
That is where the cut
begins

valley eyes fill red
scrape for
sober moisture

crush further than fracture
low grain television
but never played chess
another letter
Morning membrane
discharge

what was meant
imagined falls
towards abrasive
chin

## Right Reasons

I would like to see
you bypassing
morning breeze
Opening a small
flower shop

It's dawn
and I would feel
pleasant

you?

Sweater grin

## Crawl

She crawled in
top heavy sex
lost traction
I didn't do well

She didn't move
Intimidation
broken leg
lover never
called

## November Suburbia

Lent sun muted between
orange reflective glass
finding their own versions
of god

Restless commuters here too
mannequin blank stares
Teenage DNA pushers cripple
giddy attention seekers
Always anxious to turn
white trash boyfriends
into rockstar posters

Graying lovers running
window surveillance
one electrical rhythm away from
trackless black oceans
Unable, unwilling to remember
a point where footprints
refused to touch cracked sidewalks
Young girls with covered mouths
singled out somewhere
beneath soup grey
november clouds
where their voices
begin to pierce

neatly placed indifference

                    cupped hands, knee pulled to
chest

a little too much

              she notices

# Field Vision

Red veins morph into frigid plastic
electrical impulses run through the processor
to the utility which accepts orders
Valves keep the transmission of essential fluids
flowing through the unconscious machine
The system excites with a rush of chemical
coattails,
fools itself into believing in life
Buried under a webbing of wires and insulation,
a light blue spark deviates from predestined
channels
Adrenaline, endorphins, testosterone line up to
create
a polysynthetic barrier
The Small spark hurdles itself into the obstacle,
gaining freedom to speed beyond the circuits
This field, protected by massive grey buildings,
lends itself to flesh and chemical
Vibrant winged relics cheer beyond the air
The concrete softens as it
becomes held up by the dying trees
And, for a brief, eternal second
the mechanics of us
fail to express emotion

## A Bit Dizzy

It's the feeling of going to bed
wondering which apparitions
will be hovering at post
Nights of reading theologians and atheists,
their arguments beautiful and elegant,
but far from complete
Dealing with bardos of death
a possibility of rebirth
Losing my ego in a great
junction of existence
It's a bit too much
and still incomplete

And to live again?
So much regret in this life, so many dealings
fucked up because of fear or misread
eye movement
It's the bad taste of good wine
in the coughing morning
It's the unspoken moments
mistreated
and very incomplete
Something more
there has to be
But I'm not in the position
to figure this out alone

No one wants to talk,
just stare blindly into brown glass retreats
I have mine
and lean on it with a Baptist's conviction

it's looking back years later
something could have been done differently
Something less coded
something more connected

Something more connected

The day can break, left side still sore
The night can bring spirits of a different nature
drunken, obsolete, alone
It boils down to the distance
of seconds
mold devours dough into years
Maybe nothing more than
a synapse that will not release its
bite, still
that is incomplete

This naked frame is my own
egotistical, ashamed, and frantic
with urges against moral barriers
A short match, a burnt finger
A moment of bravery and years

of cowardice decay
imperfect as that shivering mass of nude flesh
nothing more perfect
Is it a ghost in a machine,
our machines are in disrepair
hunted, beaten
only given reprieve
by those times
where lips tingled
a smile occurred

And that is where
the unity of the void
and meaning join
into something
so complete

snapshot artist

blindfolded, unskilled

                                    malicious



There is nothing
            clever
                    cute
                            about being



that fucked up

## Chicago Transverse
## (retraction)

Saturday Morning
set out to see fields of monuments
Packed up teenage essentials
a green backpack of outdated ideals
to do what has been done by the cliché
the reckless unnamed

Must have been better days
because the roads have stretched into
a manic underbelly,
stained by the advertisement Newscasts
and liquor store outlet mall reality
overhead, self taken
myspace glamour shots

Only mode of flight, breaking apart
from soccer mom unwanted eyes drawing
in close the cluttered pavement which
stole the muffler

The Shouts of a new routine chisel into skull
until there are only thoughts of retraction
back to the embryo warm suspension
of non-negotiated pattern

Realizing yesterday's monuments
have been traded
for experiences that arrive tardy
when a world becomes a shopping cart
everyone shoving their way through
until they become
their own stone tributes

**Insomnia**

milk white eyelid
closed bare mossy
growth

Sleep in again
red digital reminder
fine cat exterior stretch
shower, tylenol pm

bite fist, pound headboard
sunrise again
acrylic paint dry
lullaby

## Chlorophyll

plastic bottle secret
concealed in a
low light class
an offered ride
brown haired
distraction
before the turn
oh dear
I crashed my car

Call my lawyer

My tiny
emergency exit

the reminisce of a beard
slain tremoring in
dried toothpaste
bathroom sink

I never told the truth
in order to keep
the painted chain
between where
the door never
met the wall

## Foreshadow of Stalled Events

The road nested against
the painted desert
underneath your
tree bark iris
and beneath
your chest

this can't linger
each time it
re-configures into
another night
hopping into
hobbling into
one bar into
the next into
neon nonsense

somehow
my car makes
its way into the absent
space absent of
flashing lights
the hammer ready
to fall

it has been 96 days

since we shared
a pillow and 36 days
since I ran about
Boston, gin soaked
making my way
to another brick stained
encounter

stand up for once
that has been said
but an absent bed
absent notions
a digital picture
that I can't stare
at anymore tonight

so lets take this drive
just admire
mute exhaustion
for a moment
I don't have time
for these
dodge and miss games
alarm clock
ringing us back
to glazed stare
reality

They are all very nice

but I get off on friction

just like everyone else

## Whiskey Knife

Another bottle
goes down
in a wet glass graveyard
of busted telephones,
burnt notes where
their dejections
are only of the
kindest nature

insincere

Sick just the same
ill by nature
a reputation
of imperfection

Preemptive strikes
against the egg shell
emotions.
A semi gloss handjob
It's no ones fault
if a staggered meeting
at the door step
led to uncovering
the antagonist
erected hours before

Back to the cage
and rewind misses
black out kisses
against a rotting
set design
an opportunity
in flight, back imprinted
carpet patterns,
rug burn procreation
Another bottle
a technical vagina
The final
graveyard

# Airline

Torn up cereal box whore
saved in fuselage
islands of continuity floating
towards something great

Quick trip to someplace warm
broken elevation
stain tooth smile
during turbulence
nothing can frighten me
two hours of engine noise
rest in Detroit

Cleveland closed
Boston wasted
Tampa underwater
Circle around patchwork landscape
numbness

## Overt Flirtation

Another hand closer
from tunnels too deep
be prepared for an air raid
sell plasma for a bomb hatch

no need for anger
it won't leave you
with many friends
a mammal cannot
survive in a vacuum

do her dreams bite down
like yellow striped candy?
very pretty

Did I say anything meaningful?
I am not sure
I woke up trembling

## RadioTransmissionApology

Every bit in constant flux

Each moment complex
negotiations between the
mind and instinct content
in every muscle movement
released underneath
the umbrella
her tiny fingers
gripped plastic, a cloth
shelter from the arena
she once danced
when I was sober

But the rain makes
the lines starker and
it doesn't conceal
the evidence of
this guilt and
torn chest regret

The eyes that
never will read this
A frequency of apology
without transmitter
And while each cell

exchanges with the body
flesh, timid
regroups

Then perhaps
a portion of this will
find its way through
the millennia
then the physical
will realize the metaphorical
space between
your fingers and the
small plastic handle of
your umbrella

politicos' anthropology


devolution


How can I write about war?




I have never been there

## Lady Luck Gin Lips

It's the best kind
of luck, the best
kind of destructive
affair
court costs and
lawyer fees escaping
breath with manly
arm pump

Lock up, not for me
The glass eye dropped
tongue bit held steady
nail break hands slept
inch thick plastic urine
stained mat
the more coherent
yelping in an 8 inch
block of bash taking
shit kicking
fuck heads.

Sing again, to myself
how I move, one step
to the next, laughing
Head cocked immunity
all the best cards played

distraction, heavy hours
Where was the old lady Gin,
the things that could have been
if I didn't cheat her
red blue nasty
morning, handcuffs
and judges

I'm on
both knees, flowers in
hand

Then again, a new routine
a nice spot of
correspondence,
let this go. go. go.
little go go dancer
she won't see the day
shimmy back
down their tube.
a summer trashed

the best kind of luck
the best kind of
destructive affair

swine fed
     self feed

    money in hand


     female
black eyed fodder

things we witness cruel

    I cannot change
any of this
      consciousness begets consciousness
potassium keeps the heart going

## American Caricature

I must be an American caricature
cartoon cigarette dropped
below the chin
hands clinched
around the wheel
going eighty in a forty-five
a flashlight between my legs
pin point words of what
was said the night before
the moment I fortified
with beating muscle
and began the retreat
into bedroom entrances
they would never see

10pm Wednesday

The television
shot it's silent propaganda
black and white
film noir
half bottle of Hennessy
then that special ring
just for, something
wait, I really need
to start again

a phone call?
that's a bad penny
that's hitting 22

I must be the American fool
forgotten amongst the strangest
alpha males and scowling
comments set forth from
friends more interested
that I am not sleeping alone
I sleep alone drainage ditch
hotel lobbies and absent
pillows perfumed by
other moments I can't recall

11pm Wednesday
The television is off
the phone is dead
I killed it against the wall
nail marked palms
wait, again,
this is an exaggeration
I don't remember

I am an American romantic
rushed in cowboy form
bowed out early
syndicated laugh track

used from teen comedies
half wit dramas
prom dresses I never saw

12am Thursday

resolution restoration
unloading inadequacies
like bricks on uneasy
bar flies
old man fishing hat
that is you, a worn
out silhouette
broken down car
but I haven't written in months
nothing worthwhile
an hour at the pub
and broken pen
car keys clinched wrapped around
silly flirtation one eye closed
to maintain focus

I must be a midwestern loser
stuck in a dunk tank
of rumors
never given time
to mend
I should have apologized

but for whose sake?
Social webbing
my feet stick
dim brown flashlight bulb
incased in aluminum
crystal palace
to see in the dark

7am one month later
missed the call from
the other coast

I must be an American caricature
a lit cigarette
a missed train
hands clinched
around the wheel
going eighty in a forty-five

This cartoon life
is getting to me

## Table Gum

Sometimes I sit and watch
the way couple's feet
move in unison
as if there was something sticky
keeping them together

## Morning Paper

Pupils tear off each
section, silly putty
third person gossip

each threat, a pick up line
for every caffeine laced
thick framed glasses
elitist

chain store punditry
reactionary to everybody
but most things
compromise

polarized

each setting, an opportunity
to create witty noise
Exactly that
indiscernible pitch notes
spikes interrupting low
ink tone buzzing

So long to the ketamine kids

        the plastic scent of
        sexcapades

farewell good chemicals
                ms contin couch sitters

silence listening to thought

## Pinhole Viewpoint

Sulked far from
hand held museum
oddities
antiquity brought upon
fresh by
bristled contact
each line indistinguishable
from a pinhole view
A cold car quick touch
against an elevator ride
taxi cab embrace
misdirection
that burnt everything
good in the chest
only to sweep the flames
with apathy

Disgusted by
charred fingers
you
shrug back
unpronounced

## At Our Best

Pollen infested swarms
bring back longer days
with neglected televisions
and muddy shoes

hair made to
soldier straight
at attention
when snap singularity
envelopes the crowd

absence of gravity
as each other courses
in each other
up the spinal cord
and radiates with intent
pouring collision
through mosaic
glass shell ambiance

## 114 North

steady white lines
through overpass guardians
a busted radio
a day old strawberry milkshake
funneled out highway momentum
down 114 where I kept my fakes
those who would steer me further just
to see the crash, metal bent, rust worn
given enough steam, all things decay

I wanted to stop her
put her in slow motion and
follow through
She would rather be in film
tinted stark screen
where it rains and
nobody sleeps through
the climax

No climax
just a string
of repetition
tire marks and bad
breaks

It's enough to
be doing well
and concentrate
on white noise mantras

then again, I need more
than a skip beat mummer
a day old milkshake

pt.2
(inside)

I can't stand her because she leaves at 2am

engine start reminder
every single time

the world shuts down
four hours prior in
towns like these

Living room television glow
silver flickers
each viewer
takes to bed
sick world broadcasts

others here;
they stay up
later

some just can't sleep
turn to t.v.

memory imprints
after image effect

2am the reception is poor
the street is quiet
snow freezes
dry static

## Mantis

Swallow down to the neck
that is how the evidence is lost

Know what I have built

Barriers
Barricades

Protect the warmth at all cost
Who needs sleep when
we have television?

Cut the fidgety finger at the tip
a surprisingly friendly girl
another tongue in my mouth

An amazing dilemma
I became the boyish head
bobbing in the river

## The Epitome of Her

on the floor
      shame, honey, wax
fall down
      stretch neck cigarette
it finds you by
instinct and un-burnt letters
takes you in
while brushing
hair past slow
shift, flow

      out of the tenth window
      up at the tenth floor

it sighs and wakes you
before the ground

## Planet Crash

It's alright dying
but better to move again
not focused
run and gun
mating
awkward
biology glances

Needlehead angels
can give something nice
not as good
as disarmed relaxation

the world stops
from agitation
inability to
seize the whole
just a body fighting
against itself

a deluge of breathing
an honest handshake
better an embrace
that slices through
membrane violence

better to understand
the disillusion that
is the
will to
power
fallacy

wicked little kids
run ruin the world
it's better to stumble
towards neighbor
past shadow of self

## EXIT /END

conveniently timed amnesia
songs of color blindness
spinning gin dizzy
to sirens of tinnitus

with all sincerity

everything is alright

the objects received
returned to shelves
amongst playthings

a world recreated
with the potentiality
of a glance

www.ingramcontent.com/pod-product-compliance
Lightning Source LLC
Chambersburg PA
CBHW020521030426
42337CB00011B/501